Milk Soapmaking
The Smart and Simple Guide to Making Lovely Milk Soap From Cow Milk, Goat Milk, Buttermilk, Cream, Coconut Milk, or Any Other Animal or Plant Milk

— Anne L. Watson —

Anne L. Watson's *Smart Soapmaking* was the first book based on modern techniques that eliminate the drudgery and guess-work from home soapmaking. Now, by popular demand, she continues her soapmaking revolution with the first practical, comprehensive book on making milk soap.

Experience the rich, soothing, luxurious feel of milk soap you've made yourself. Your skin will thank you for it.

"Beautiful in its simplicity. . . . A definitive book for experienced as well as beginning milk soapers."

Rebekah Bailey, The Original Soap Dish
South Whitley, Indiana

"An easy to read and understand book that will take the mystery out of milk-based soapmaking."

Amanda Guilfoyle
Bodelicious Bath & Body Products
Ipswich, Queensland, Australia

"If you have an interest in milk soaps, this is the book for you. . . . Debunks much of the popular wisdom that may have discouraged some soapmakers."

Kevin M. Dunn
Author, *Caveman Chemistry* and
***Scientific Soapmaking* (forthcoming)**

Milk Soapmaking

The Smart and Simple Guide to Making Lovely Milk Soap From Cow Milk, Goat Milk, Buttermilk, Cream, Coconut Milk, or Any Other Animal or Plant Milk

Anne L. Watson

Shepard Publications
Olympia, Washington

Illustrations by Wendy Edelson, www.wendyedelson.com
Back cover photo by Aaron Shepard

ISBN 978-0-938497-45-5

Library of Congress Control Number: 2008937070
Library of Congress subject heading: Soap

Version 1.0

*For Georgyee and Jim,
my mom and dad*

Contents

Acknowledgments

Susan Kennedy of Oregon Trail Soap Supplies gave me a great deal of help and advice when I first learned to make milk soap. So, I'd like to thank her particularly for getting me started.

Special thanks to Laurie Drake, Amanda Guilfoyle, Deena Humphrey, Ruth Kohl, and Marge Robbins for their milk soap recipes.

To Connie Rutter, Sister Angela Hoffman, and Kevin M. Dunn, who gave me chemists' views on soapmaking.

To the testers and/or commenters: Dawn Blakey, Laurie Drake, Deborah Everett, Katherine Gee, Amanda Guilfoyle, Pip Guyatt, Randie Hilliard, Deena Humphrey, Christine Keiser, Kevin Knabe, Ruth Kohl, Beth Milton, Carol Noski, Pat Potter, Marge Robbins, Carol Schatz, and Julie Seismore.

To Rebekah Bailey of The Original Soap Dish and to Anne-Marie Faiola and her staff at Bramble Berry Soap Making Supplies for sharing information on materials and methods.

And especially to my husband, Aaron Shepard, who edited, designed, and published this book.

A Few First Thoughts

Since my book *Smart Soapmaking* was published, I've been asked again and again if it covers milk soapmaking. It doesn't. Milk soapmaking is a subject unto itself. It uses different materials, of course, but besides that, it needs a different approach. Too much material to cram into one book, I felt.

Also, milk soaps weren't my specialty at that time. I'd made a few, and they were fine soaps. In fact, several people who received bars of my whipping cream soap as gifts began to nag me to go back into the soap business. But I didn't consider myself an expert.

Time changes things. As I started trying to answer questions from soapmakers about milk soap, I was drawn farther and farther into the subject. I learned about the different types of milk, what to expect from them, and how to handle each one.

I made hundreds of bars of soap from dozens of different recipes. I experimented with scent and color to see what happens when they're used with milk. Then there were non-dairy milks to consider—would any of them make good soap? On a spreadsheet, I kept a log of my experiments—what went into each batch, and what came out.

When I got unexpected results, I asked materials vendors and chemists—*what's going on here*? And they were kind enough to tell me, so a few more puzzle pieces snapped into place. Then I set up a testing program, giving and sending out soap sets identified only by number to testers who rated them for lather, feel, and general attractiveness.

In the end, I decided to write another book. Otherwise, I really would have had to go back into the soap business.

Myths and Milk

Stories You Hear About Milk Soapmaking

Readers of my first soap book, *Smart Soapmaking,* know I collect soapmaking myths. Here are a few about *milk* soapmaking.

Myth #1: Only an experienced soapmaker should try it.

"You can't learn milk soapmaking until you're adept at making water-based soaps."

I'm sorry to admit, I've said this myself. The reason I bought this tale was that one of the few soapmaking failures of my life till then was a batch of milk soap. I followed all the directions in the recipe and ended up with soap that was studded with undissolved nuggets of lye. Definitely *not* recommended as a beauty treatment!

So, I used to say that it's best to avoid milk soaps until you're more experienced with soapmaking. But after a couple of soapmakers told me they'd learned just fine on milk soaps, I reconsidered. Why should I have to know about one kind of soap to make another?

What had made my batch fail wasn't lack of experience with water-based soaps—it was a lack of precise, science-based instructions for *milk* soap. Even on the very first batch, a novice should be able to succeed if such instructions were available. It's just that they haven't been—until now!

Myth #2: Milk soaps are especially difficult.

"Milk is so temperamental in soapmaking, it's easy to end up with a total disaster."

This myth is related to Myth #1 and contains as little truth. Supposedly, the inherent difficulty of milk soaps means that the uninitiated shouldn't even try.

But to me, "temperamental" means, even if you do everything properly, you might fail anyway. This isn't true with milk soaps. Do everything right, and there's little chance of your soap not turning out well.

There's the catch—do everything right. After dozens of experiments for this book, including some pretty spectacular failures, I identified what caused problems and how to avoid them.

Here's the solution: I found there are two good ways to make milk soaps. But neither is good for all *kinds* of milk. In fact, if one technique works, the other probably won't. The key to success is to choose the right technique for the milk you want to use. I'll tell you how to do that.

Making milk soap *does* require some tricks. But, as any stage magician can tell you, a trick explained is merely a procedure.

Myth #3: Goat milk is superior to cow.

"Goat milk is far better for soapmaking because it's much higher in fat than cow, and the fat globules are smaller."

Whether goat milk is higher in fat depends on several factors—the breeds of goat and cow, points in their lactation cycles, what the animals eat, and whether the milk is straight from the farm or is processed commercially. The cartoned goat milk in my local supermarket is *lower* in fat than commercial whole milk from cows. Commercial goat dairies remove a lot of the cream for cheesemaking.

There are numerous differences between goat milk and cow, and it's true that the average size of the fat globules of goat milk is smaller. But regardless of chemical differences, the real test of a soap comes when you wash with it.

So, for this book, I made dozens of batches of soap from all kinds of milk. Each batch was recorded in a log and identified with a number. I gave samples to over a dozen testers, with requests to compare the soaps.

These testers didn't favor goat milk soap over cow. The only patterns I could see were that they mostly favored fluid milk over powdered or evaporated, and that they slightly favored farm milk over commercial.

So, if you can't get goat milk where you live, don't worry. You can still make great soap!

Myth #4: The milk must be pasteurized.

"Farm milk isn't safe to use for soapmaking unless you pasteurize it yourself."

I asked a microbiologist for facts on this one. She said, "Lye kills cells, and that includes germ cells. There's no reason to pasteurize milk before you make soap with it."

Some of my tests used unpasteurized milk, and others used pasteurized (in some countries called *sterilized*). If there was any difference in quality, it wasn't enough for me to notice.

Myth #5: Only animal milks will work.

"If you're allergic to animal milk, or you're a vegan, forget about milk soap."

I tested all the kinds of plant milk I could get my hands on. Some didn't make good soap, but others were great. So, I've included instructions for those too.

Myth #6: Only whole milk and cream should be used for soapmaking.

"You can't make good soap with lowfat or nonfat milk."

This one is a real puzzler. Considering that water, the more common liquid used in soapmaking, is *completely* "nonfat," I don't see the logic. And yes, I've made fine, creamy soap with ordinary nonfat dry milk.

Moisturizing and richness in soaps is partly due to the recipe's *superfatting*—fat added beyond what's needed to neutralize the lye. It also depends on what fat is used. The fat in milk is only one kind of fat in the soap, and just a small portion of the total fat.

Butterfat *does* make pleasant soap, and soaps made with cream are indeed rich and creamy. My test bars with these ingredients lathered lavishly—and didn't last as long as most soaps, or produce satisfactory results with fancy molds. So, there are advantages and disadvantages.

The notion that lower-fat products can't be used for soapmaking could have originated with soapmakers who weren't using stick blenders. Lowfat milks may get lumpy when the lye is first added, and without a stick blender, they may not produce a smooth soap.

Given the tools we're using today, the milk you choose is a matter of taste. You may find you prefer the cream-based soaps for bathing and facial soaps, while buttermilk or other lowfat-milk soap may meet your needs for hand washing.

Whatever you do—experiment. Don't let anyone else tell you what you like. It's well worth your time and effort to find out for yourself!

What Is Milk Soap, Anyway?
What It Is and What Goes Into It

Soap is formed by combining fat with lye. If you add milk while making it, it becomes *milk soap. Milk*—if you'll excuse my stretch—here means any dairy product that's liquid or semi-liquid (or dried from one of those into a powder), along with any milky liquid made from plants.

Let's look at all this more closely. When you mix an acid with a base, a chemical reaction takes place. A familiar example of this is combining baking soda and vinegar.

A special form of this type of reaction occurs when the acids in the mixture are fatty acids such as contained in all oils and butters. When a strong base such as lye is mixed with these fats, soap is produced. The reaction that causes that is called *saponification.*

When you add milk to the recipe, you're working with a mixture that also includes proteins and sugars. They affect the quality of the soap in ways I'll point out as we go along. Having these ingredients in the picture does give you more to watch out for. But there's nothing hard about it, and I'll show you how to allow for it.

This book covers *cold process* milk soapmaking. *Cold process* (CP) is a general soapmaking method, and probably the most common. Most often, there's nothing actually "cold" about it, but it's called that because ingredients are not heated or cooked after mixing.

Now let's look in detail at what goes into milk soap. (For even more on soapmaking ingredients in general, see my book *Smart Soapmaking*.)

Milks

Milk for soapmaking comes in many forms and from many sources. Here are the most common.

Farm milk. I use this term to mean milk coming straight from the animal without processing. Though you may not have livestock of your own, you might find a small dairy selling milk directly to customers. In some places, this might not be possible if sale of unpasteurized milk is illegal. But in other places, laws might forbid selling it as food but still allow selling to soapmakers. A farm might even supply animal milk not normally sold—sheep, donkey, horse, camel, yak, llama, or . . . ?

Commercial milk. As packaged by commercial dairies, both cow and goat milk have a standardized fat content, one that's lower than you might find if you buy from a farm.

Cream. One way to make sure your milk produces creamy soap is to use cream itself. (This does *not* include whipped cream from an aerosol can!) If you're near a goat farm, you can probably get goat cream—a cream layer does rise on goat milk, contrary to what you might have heard.

Cream acts a little differently than other fluid dairy products, and I'll point out the differences in my instructions. Give cream-based soaps a little extra time to cure—they tend to be a bit sticky when first unmolded.

Cream comes with a wide range of butterfat content, and with different names according to that content. Both the percentages and the names can vary with the country you live in. For instance, one of my recipes calls for half-and-half, an

American product. This is simply light or single cream mixed about equally with milk to give 10% to 12% fat. If you can't buy it, you can mix it yourself in your kitchen.

Likewise, you may live where whipping cream normally comes with heavier fat content than what I recommend, which is about 30%. Cream much heavier than that can cause problems with mixing and can also produce a softer soap. So, you may want to dilute its fat content by adding milk.

Fermented milk. Buttermilk has been used in beauty treatments for centuries. It contains an alpha hydroxy acid similar to those in expensive anti-aging creams. Of course, you have to expect any acid to be neutralized by the lye in cold process soapmaking. However that may be, buttermilk makes very nice soap.

Yogurt and sour cream are similar to buttermilk in soapmaking. Both should be diluted before you add them—one part distilled water to one part yogurt or sour cream. If you don't dilute them, they may not mix properly and you may get marbled streaks through your soap.

Since fermented milks contain less sugar, the soap mixture is a bit less likely to overheat or discolor.

Evaporated milk. This milk is higher in fat, protein, and sugar than fresh milk is. It's also darker-colored. If it's not diluted, it will make a relatively dark soap.

To some of my testers, evaporated milk soap seemed the least desirable type. But one said it felt richer and had better lather than an otherwise identical soap made with regular commercial milk.

Powdered milk. Powdered (dehydrated) cow or goat milk is easy to find and store. It makes fine soap, as long as you handle it in such a way that it doesn't separate out of the mixture—as I'll later explain.

There are quite a few kinds of powdered milk, some made for the kitchen, others marketed to backpackers. One kind I *don't* recommend is non-instant whole powdered cow milk. I've made successful batches with it, but it's caused more than its share of failures. If you do work with it, you must be especially careful about temperatures and mixing. Otherwise, you may wind up with undissolved milk in the soap.

The best way to tell if a powdered milk will work is to look at the instructions for reconstituting it. If it has to be mixed with hot water, it may not dissolve easily in your soap mixture. If you still want to use it, the safest thing to do is reconstitute it according to the directions and treat it like any other fluid milk.

Plant milks. These include soy, coconut, rice, and almond. All of these can be purchased, and some you can make yourself. I'll discuss them in detail in a later chapter.

Fats

Soapmaking fat comes from both animal and plant sources. Mineral oils cannot be used to make soap.

Soapmakers differ about using animal fat. Tallow and lard make good, inexpensive soap, but if you're opposed to their use, you can choose from many excellent fats made from plants.

Fats can be solid or liquid—referring to their state at room temperature. Solid fats include tallow, lard, shea butter, coconut oil, avocado butter, and many others. Some solid fats occur naturally, others are made by artificial hydrogenation of oils.

The liquid fats include all the cooking and salad oils, as well as shea oil, castor oil, and the oil of numerous other seeds—from flax seed to peach pits. A few of the liquid fats are made by removing some of the fatty acids from normally solid fats. Examples of this include shea oil and fractionated coconut oil. In the past, these have not been used much in soapmaking, but I've found they can make great soap.

Basic oils such as corn, safflower, olive, and coconut are sold by grocery stores, health food stores, food co-ops, restaurant suppliers, and big-box discount stores.

Exotic oils and almost all butters will probably have to be bought from stores that sell soapmaking supplies, or from catalogs or Internet sources. You may find just what you're looking for from a small supplier that serves a special market niche. Though catalogs and Internet sources may sell basic oils as well, and at lower prices, buying those locally may still be cheaper, since you avoid shipping costs.

Any grocery store will offer vegetable shortening, a solid fat that is most often a blend of inexpensive oils, mostly hydrogenated. While I don't recommend this as food, it's good for making milk soaps!

Shortening is usually sold under recognizable brand names, which vary by country. For instance, two of my recipes call for Crisco, a soy/cottonseed oil blend that is the most popular American brand. Can you substitute a different one? You normally can't just replace one fat with another in a recipe due to differing lye requirements—but the requirements for soy and cottonseed are almost identical, so you can safely use any other shortening made from those two oils without worrying about differing proportions. Corn oil added to the blend is also safe, though soap properties may then change. But you shouldn't substitute a brand with large amounts of palm oil or any coconut oil unless you know how to recalculate the recipe.

Lye

Besides fat, the other most important ingredient in soapmaking is lye. This name can actually refer to any of several alkalis—a kind of strong *base,* the opposite of an acid—and it can even refer to those alkalis plus the water they're dissolved in. But nowadays "lye" almost always means the dry form of sodium hydroxide, or caustic soda—and that's what you'll use in your soapmaking. (Liquid soap, by the way, takes a different kind of lye—potassium hydroxide, or caustic potash.)

Formerly, lye was readily available in grocery stores—but in some communities it has been taken off the shelves because it's used in making not only soap but also illegal drugs. You might find it at a hardware or home improvement store (DIY store, in the U.K.). If not, chemical suppliers may sell small quantities. Or buy from soapmaking supply Web sites or from other soapmakers.

The label should say "100% lye" or "100% sodium hydroxide." Never use a drain cleaning product that doesn't give this assurance, because otherwise the lye may be combined with ingredients you can't use in soapmaking.

Lye comes in two common forms: flake and bead. I've tried them both, and found that each has advantages and drawbacks.

Flake lye is the most pleasant to use. There's little if any tendency for the large, thin flakes to scatter as you pour and weigh. But it does not dissolve well in cold or high-fat liquids, and that applies to many milk soaps. Don't even try it if your recipe has cream.

Bead lye can be used for all soapmaking, including for milk soaps. This kind of lye does dissolve in cold and high-fat liquids, but you have to pay special attention to make sure of it.

That was the reason for my early failed batch of milk soap—the lye didn't dissolve completely. (I've since found a scientific way to determine whether lye is dissolved even when you can't see through the liquid, and I'll share this with you.)

You're extremely unlikely to burn yourself or anyone else with lye if you just follow directions, pay attention, and use gloves and goggles as I'll recommend. But if it does happen, flush the burn with cold running water for at least fifteen minutes, with any contaminated clothing removed. Lye manufacturers recommend that you then call a doctor or poison control center for further help.

Water

Water isn't the principal liquid in milk soaps, but it can be used to dilute yogurt, sour cream, or evaporated milk, or to reconstitute powdered milk. I recommend distilled water, since tap or well water may cause soap to fail.

Other Liquids

It's possible to reconstitute powdered milk in liquids other than water—in an herbal tea, for example. It's a tempting idea, but one that may introduce a "wild card" into your soap. I'm not saying it's impossible, or even difficult, to formulate a good soap with tea. But it may take a bit of trial and error to end up with what you want.

Additives

Probably the most common soap additive is scent. You might expect milk soaps to have a natural milky scent, but as a rule, they don't. The soapmaking process destroys most of the scent, and the little that remains doesn't usually last.

So, scents are often added. The two kinds used most often are *essential oils* and *fragrance oils*.

An e*ssential oil* is an aromatic oil produced from a plant, sometimes diluted with a carrier oil. Some soapmakers prefer essential oils because they're "natural." However, some people are allergic to particular ones. Some essential oils are not recommended for use during pregnancy. Some don't work well in soap—for example, the scent of citrus essential oils tends to fade quickly.

A few essential oils may affect the color of soap. Citrus essential oils may change it, as may patchouli, German chamomile, and any essential oil with a pronounced yellow tone. However, most won't. So, if you're trying for very pale colors with your milk soaps, essential oils may be the best choice.

Research the properties of any essential oil you find appealing, and start with a small test batch to make sure the result pleases you. Or you might just use lavender, since it's pleasant, available, and generally safe. I've never used a lavender essential oil that affected the color.

Essential oils are available from grocery stores, health food stores, food co-ops, New Age stores, soapmaking supply stores, and Internet sources. Almost all of these except Internet sources sell small quantities at high prices. This is fine for your first batch or two, but after that, save money by checking the Internet. Search on the keywords "essential oils soapmaking" for a long list of suppliers.

A *fragrance oil* is an artificial chemical aroma in a carrier oil. Fragrance oils are supposed to be nontoxic, but like essential oils, they may sometimes cause allergic reactions. *Un*like some essential oils, they don't fade quickly.

A major consideration with fragrance oils is that many will darken or discolor milk soap at least a little. The vendor may not mention it, because it wouldn't be important in general soapmaking. But if a whitish or cream-colored soap is what you want, you'll either have to test a fragrance or contact the vendor before buying it to ask about minor color change.

Actually, even pronounced color change may not be mentioned unless you ask. Sometimes, such changes take several days to develop and may start out looking horrible, but may then improve considerably. I had one fragrance turn a batch of soap meaty red, so I threw out most of it. But within a few days, the bars I kept became an acceptable, if not especially beautiful, reddish brown. So, don't be too quick to give up if your soap color turns funny-looking.

Many Internet sources sell fragrance oils. But before you buy one, make sure it's suitable for cold process soap. The seller should state that prominently.

When you open a bottle of essential oil or fragrance oil, especially for the first time, keep the opening turned away from you and/or wear goggles. Once in a long while, the oil from one of these bottles sprays all over.

Another common soap additive is colorant. Colorants don't always work well in milk soaps. For one thing, milk soaps are rarely white to start with. They vary in color with the type of milk. So a colorant is building on a base that has its own color, and the results may be odd.

You'll need to experiment to make sure a particular colorant works well in a particular recipe. Milk soaps may darken over a couple of weeks, so let them cure before you decide.

One additive that needs special mention is titanium dioxide. This is a white pigment commonly used to override the natural creamy-to-beige color of milk soaps, at least partly. This might give you a prettier soap when you're adding colorants, but there's a tradeoff: Titanium dioxide reduces lather and moisturizing significantly.

Other additives may be used to make the soap harder, make it more moisturizing, increase abrasiveness—you name it. Possibilities include food products such as oatmeal and poppy seed, minerals such as mica and pumice, and decorative or therapeutic flowers and herbs.

Some additives—particularly whole plant materials like lavender buds—don't come out of a lye bath looking as pretty as when they went in. So, find out how well a particular additive works before you make a big batch with it.

What Do I Use to Make It?
Gathering the Equipment You Need

Essential equipment for soapmaking includes a scale for measuring correctly, a thermometer for checking the temperature, and a stick blender for proper mixing. You may already have these tools in your kitchen.

The scale should be digital and should weigh in tenths of an ounce, or in grams, or in both. A good postal scale will do fine and shouldn't be expensive. Such scales are available from office supply stores or on the Web.

Your scale should have a button or other control to adjust

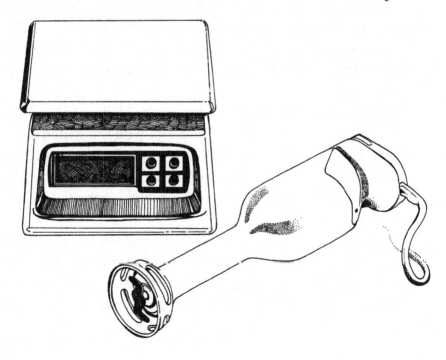

for *tare*—the weight of the container. Before filling a container, place it empty on the scale and push the tare button. The scale will reset to zero. (You may have to push the tare button more than once to make that happen.) Now, when you put in your ingredients, you'll get their weight without the container's.

You'll need a waterproof, "instant-read" digital food thermometer, because temperature is especially important in milk soapmaking. To get good results, you must keep temperatures within certain ranges, depending on what kind of milk you're using. Also, your thermometer will tell you when your lye is properly dissolved. A second food thermometer might be handy too, but that one doesn't need to be digital.

A stick blender is important for any cold process soapmaking, but even more so for making milk soap. Lye can turn milk protein grainy, and a stick blender will correct this.

If you haven't used a stick blender before, take time to learn how it works before you make soap with it. As a safety feature, the power switch must be held in the "on" position for the blender to run. Whenever you let up on the switch, the blade stops.

Try it out first with water. Lower the blade into the liquid before turning on the blender, then let up on the switch before lifting the blade back out. The blade must not be turning as it enters or leaves the liquid, or else the liquid might splatter. Practice until you can handle the switch correctly without thinking.

Protective gloves and goggles are absolutely essential for safety. Many soapmakers recommend the rubber gloves sold for cleaning and dishwashing. I also like the extra-long gloves you buy in paint stores to wear while stripping furniture. It's best to use gloves that fit snugly. This may mean choosing a size smaller than you wear for dishwashing.

Your gloves will probably cut down on your dexterity, so take extra care and watch your hands. If the gloves make it hard to press buttons on your scale or microwave, use your knuckle instead of your fingertip.

Goggles should be the snug-fitting kind worn by wood-workers. Glasses or sunglasses, even the wraparound kind, aren't good enough. Don't take the slightest risk with your eyes. Any hardware store should sell the kind of goggles you need, and they're not expensive.

The instructions in this book call for a microwave oven to melt solid fat. Though that's best, you could melt it instead in a slow cooker, or in a regular oven at the lowest possible heat.

You also need the following kitchenware:

• Soup pot, stainless steel or enameled steel spatterware, or other large pot. Don't use aluminum—it reacts chemically with lye and may be unsafe. My pot holds about eight quarts (about eight liters), which for my recipes leaves a good distance between the surface of the soap and the top of the pot. Since the soap mixture must be deep enough to keep the blade of the stick blender submerged, the pot should have a diameter of no more than about eight inches (about twenty centimeters) for recipes of the size in this book.

• Saucepan, stainless steel. One that holds two quarts (or two liters) is ideal. You could use enameled steel, but it won't work quite as well, as I'll explain later.

• Large microwave-safe bowl or glass measuring pitcher (large jug, in the U.K.). I prefer a pitcher because I like having the handle and pour spout. Mine holds 10 cups (about two liters). Plastic is fine if it's microwave-safe.

• Bowls, pitchers, or measuring cups for weighing lye, fat, and milk powder. Quart-size (or liter-size) is perfect for the fat, while about half that size is good for the lye. For lye, I strongly prefer a stainless steel container, because it eliminates static electricity, minimizing the amount of lye dispersed through the air.

• Two long-handled spoons for stirring—steel, stainless steel, or plastic. For the one used to stir the lye solution, the best choice is a slotted spoon.

• For some recipes, you'll need a dishpan, roasting pan (stainless or enameled steel), or similar container that your saucepan can sit in with room on all sides. This is for a water bath to cool the lye solution. It's also helpful to have a small metal trivet or rack to raise your saucepan so the water can get underneath.

• For other recipes, a small sieve.

• Miscellaneous equipment and supplies, such as an ice cube tray, a plastic dishpan, a rubber or silicone spatula, small bowls, paper towels, and vinegar.

• A tray mold, or six to eight individual bar molds. A tray mold might be a commercial soap mold, with or without dividers, or it could be a box, a tin, a food container, or a cake pan. For the recipes in this book, your mold should hold at least five cups (1.2 l), and the area of its bottom should be about 64 square inches (about 400 sq cm). (To get the area of a square or rectangle, multiply its length by its width.)

If you use individual bar molds, make sure their combined volume is about the same as for a tray mold. You can also use semi-disposable food storage containers (originally marketed in the U.S. as GladWare) or other containers, just as long as they'll hold all your soap.

If milk soap in a large mold is deeper than about an inch (about two and a half centimeters), the color is likely to turn out splotchy. So, even if your tray mold has enough volume to hold any excess, it's good to have a couple of bar molds handy to take care of that instead.

I'll say much more about molds in a later chapter.

One more thing you'll need is something to test your finished soap for excess lye. I strongly recommend pH strips, which measure degrees of acidity or alkalinity. Brought in contact with the soap, they change color. Match that color to one on the chart that comes with the strips, and you have your measurement. (I'll also say more later about how to test.)

The most important thing to know about pH strips is that there are several kinds, designed to test different ranges. The strips you need for soap will test in a pH range at least from 7 (neutral) to 11 (too alkaline to use). You can buy such strips from an Internet soapmaking supplier or from a company that sells professional or school lab supplies. Strips sold in swimming pool supply stores won't test in this range, and neither will strips used for aquariums, gardening, or saliva tests.

Different brands of pH strips have slightly different color ranges. Some should be used only under natural light, since an ordinary light bulb may shift the subtle shades of green or tan.

Got all your equipment and supplies? Let's make soap!

The Two Ways to Make Milk Soap
And How to Choose Between Them

There are two techniques for making milk soaps successfully—and they aren't interchangeable. This may be one reason why milk soaps have their reputation for being "temperamental." The technique to choose is based on the kind of milk in the recipe, and good results depend on the right choice.

Cool Technique is what you normally use with fluid milk (liquid or semi-liquid), including dry milk that has been reconstituted. In Cool Technique, the milk is weighed and frozen ahead of time. This aims to keep the milk as cold as possible so the heat of the chemical reaction won't brown the milk sugars.

Warm Technique is what you use with powdered milk that has *not* been reconstituted. In Warm Technique, the powder is blended directly into the fat. This makes sure the powder dissolves completely instead of separating out and forming a crust on top of your soap. You may also need a variation on this technique with some fluid plant milks.

Don't confuse these two techniques with *cold process* and *hot process,* two basic kinds of soapmaking. Cool Technique and Warm Technique are simply variations on cold process soapmaking that I've developed to work better for milk soaps.*

---

* Though both techniques as presented here are my own, I took my starting point for Cool Technique from tips by Susan Kennedy of Oregon Trail Soap Supplies. Thank you, Suz!

Anne's Cool Milk Soap
(Cool Technique)

Here is the recipe I recommend for your first efforts at Cool Technique soapmaking. This can be made with any animal milk, fresh or reconstituted, and with some plant milks.

It's handy to copy this recipe so you don't have to flip pages back and forth as you work through the instructions.

> 9 oz (255 g) coconut oil
> 21 oz (595 g) olive oil
> 9 oz (255 g) fluid milk (cow, goat, coconut, soy, etc.)
> 4.1 oz (116 g) lye

**Before proceeding, read the following pages
thoroughly to understand the method!**

Anne's Warm Milk Soap
(Warm Technique)

Here is the recipe I recommend for your first efforts at Warm Technique soapmaking. This can be made with any kind of powdered milk.

It's handy to copy this recipe so you don't have to flip pages back and forth as you work through the instructions.

> 9 oz (255 g) coconut oil
> 21 oz (595 g) olive oil
> 9 oz (255 g) distilled water
> 1 oz (28 g) powdered milk
> 4.1 oz (116 g) lye

Before proceeding, read the following pages thoroughly to understand the method!

Milk Soapmaking Step-by-Step
From Prep to Cleanup and Beyond

There are just a few basic steps to making soap—but they're slightly different for Cool Technique and Warm Technique.

For Cool Technique:

1. Freeze the fluid milk.
2. Prepare the fat.
3. Prepare the solution of milk and lye.
4. Mix the milk-and-lye solution with the fat.

For Warm Technique:

1. Prepare the mixture of dry milk and fat.
2. Prepare the lye solution.
3. Mix the lye solution with the milk-and-fat mixture.

Simple, right? Let's look at these procedures in detail now, including preliminaries and follow-up.

Unless marked, the instructions apply to both Cool and Warm techniques. Where they differ, you'll see side-by-side instructions with different shading, like so.

Cool Technique	Warm Technique
Instructions go here!	Instructions go here!

Preparing Fluid Milk

This is for Cool Technique only, because your milk must be weighed and frozen ahead of time.

Cool Technique	Warm Technique
1. Turn on your scale. Make sure it's set to your choice of ounces or grams.	Don't do a thing!
2. Place an empty pitcher or measuring cup on the scale and push the "tare" button to reset the scale to zero.	
3. Pour your milk into the pitcher till you have the correct weight for your recipe. If you pour too much, don't take the pan off the scale—remove excess with a spoon or small ladle.	
4. Pour your milk into an ice cube tray and put it in the freezer for the next day's soapmaking.	

Dressing for Soapmaking

Cover yourself completely for protection—long sleeves, long pants, socks, and solid shoes—using clothes you don't care about. Or wear a protective outer layer, like a lab coat. If you have long hair, tie it back.

Preparing the Work Areas

For your main work area, the most important requirement is a handy source of running water. I set up in my kitchen, where I can use the sink.

You'll also need good lighting, so you can more easily tell when your soap is ready to pour. Move a lamp into your work area if you have to. I can't stress too much the importance of good lighting.

You'll need a special work area for mixing the lye solution. The most important need in this area is good ventilation to remove fumes. Some soapmakers mix the lye outdoors, others work on a stovetop with the range hood fan running at top speed. Wherever your lye mixing area is, keep other people and pets away from it. If you work on a table that's painted or varnished, protect the surface with a tarp or other waterproof covering.

For both Warm and Cool techniques, you'll need this equipment in your main work area:

- Scale.
- Saucepan.
- Soup pot or other large pot.
- Large microwave-safe bowl or glass measuring pitcher for solid fat.
- Bowl or glass measuring cup for weighing lye.
- Bowl or glass measuring cup for weighing liquid fats. (But forget this if there's only one kind of liquid fat in the recipe. In that case, you'll weigh it in the soup pot.)
- Small bowls for weighing scent and colorant (if you're using them).

• Food thermometer, preferably waterproof, digital, "instant-read."

• Stick blender. Plug this in near the sink—to the right of it, if you're right-handed, to the left if you're a lefty. Take the same care you would with any electrical appliance near water. Use a grounded outlet, or if available, a GFI outlet—the kind with a circuit breaker and a reset button built in.

• Long-handled spoon, steel, stainless steel, or plastic.

• Spatula, rubber or silicone.

• Soap mold.

• Plastic dishpan for soiled utensils.

• All recipe ingredients (including lye).

In addition, you'll need

Cool Technique	Warm Technique
• Sieve.	• Bowl or glass measuring cup for weighing milk powder. It should have a large enough diameter that you can use your stick blender in it.

Here's what goes in the lye mixing area:

• Food thermometer. If you have only one thermometer to share between here and the main work area, place it here first. If you have two, this one has less need to be digital.

• Long-handled spoon, steel, stainless steel, or plastic—preferably slotted.

In addition, you'll need

Cool Technique	Warm Technique
Nothing more!	• Roasting pan, stainless or enameled steel, or dishpan. • Pitcher of cold or chilled tap water. • Bowl of ice cubes.

Preparing Other Ingredients

1. In your main work area, turn on the scale. Make sure it's set to your choice of ounces or grams.

2. Place the empty soup pot on the scale and push the "tare" button to reset the scale to zero. Pour the liquid fat into the pot till you have the correct weight for your recipe. If you pour too much, don't take the pot off the scale—remove excess with a spoon or small ladle.

If the recipe calls for more than one liquid fat, measure into a bowl instead of directly into the soup pot. Weigh one fat at a time and pour each in turn from the bowl into the pot, scraping the bowl with your spatula. This way, if you overshoot the measure of any one fat, you can remove some from the bowl before it gets mixed with the rest.

3. Weigh all solid fat for your recipe in the large microwave-safe bowl or glass measuring pitcher, using the same procedure described for weighing the liquid fat.

4. Heat the solid fat in your microwave till it is just melted. The exact time needed depends on the quantity and type of solid fat and also on your microwave. But it should take

only about a minute, so be careful not to overheat. The fat should not be allowed to boil or smoke.

Cool Technique	Warm Technique
5. You can leave the melted fat in the microwave to keep it out of the way—but just don't forget it there! This is one of the most common errors made by soapmakers—omitting the portion of fat waiting in the microwave.	5. Weigh the milk powder for your recipe in a bowl or glass measuring cup, using the same procedure described for weighing the fat.
6. Take your cubes of pre-weighed frozen milk from the freezer and put them in your saucepan.	6. Add a little of the melted fat from the microwave-safe bowl to the bowl or cup of milk powder. Stick blend this mixture to get rid of all lumps.
	7. Add this mixture plus all the liquid fat to the remainder of the melted fat in the microwave-safe bowl. Stick blend again to disperse the milk powder.
	8. Pour the distilled water (or other liquid) for your recipe into the saucepan, using the same procedure described for weighing the fat.

Mixing the Lye Solution

1. **PUT ON YOUR GOGGLES AND GLOVES.**

2. Still in your main work area, make sure your bowl or glass cup for measuring lye is completely dry, as is anything else that might contact the lye.

3. Put the bowl or cup on the scale, and tare it back to zero. If it's hard to work the scale buttons with gloves on, use your knuckle instead of your fingertip.

4. Weigh the lye for your recipe in the bowl or cup. Note: In rare cases, static electricity will make the lye grains scatter as they're poured. If you see this happen, spoon out the lye instead of pouring it. (You can also get rid of the static electricity ahead of time by wiping the bowl or cup with a dryer sheet.)

Cool Technique	Warm Technique
5. Take the bowl or cup of lye to your lye mixing area, along with the saucepan of frozen milk cubes.	5. Take the bowl or cup of lye to your lye mixing area, along with the distilled water or other liquid.
6. If your lye mixing area is on the stove in your kitchen, turn on your hood fan to top speed and open your windows.	6. If your lye mixing area is on the stove in your kitchen, turn on your hood fan to top speed and open your windows.
7. Add the lye to the frozen milk cubes in the saucepan, stirring carefully with the long-handled, slotted spoon. Note that a mixture of ice and liquid is *more* likely to splash than liquid alone would be. So, be sure to keep the pot at arm's length while you stir.	7. Set the saucepan in the roasting pan or dishpan. Trickle the lye gradually into the water in the saucepan, stirring constantly with the long-handled, slotted spoon. Note: You're adding lye to liquid. *Never add liquid to lye.*
	If you're working outdoors, stay

Cool Technique	Warm Technique

Cool Technique

As the lye dissolves, the ice cubes will melt. Unlike other soapmaking methods, Cool Technique usually produces very little in the way of lye fumes. All the same, it's best to have good ventilation for it.

Another reason to have good ventilation: Lye and milk protein react in a way that produces an ammonia-like smell. It's usually faint and goes away, but avoid breathing much of these fumes. But don't panic either, as many soapmakers do when they smell it. It's normal and expected in milk soapmaking.

As you mix the milk with the lye, the milk usually changes color, at least a little. Even if it turns really ugly, keep going, because it almost certainly won't stay that way.

Another thing you may see is grainy texture. I've read instructions for milk soapmaking that say to throw away your lye mixture if this happens—all is lost! It's another little myth, in fact. The graininess is caused by coagulation of proteins in

Warm Technique

upwind. If you're in your kitchen, stand away from the solution, keep the vent fan running, and keep the windows open. Some people are unusually sensitive to lye fumes, and no one finds them pleasant. Most people won't have a problem with the fumes from a small batch like the ones from my recipes. Just don't get too close to it or let the fumes collect.

Try to keep the lye from forming a crust on the bottom of the saucepan. You want the lye to dissolve as you add it. If a crust does form, grate it with the back of the slotted spoon. Be careful not to splash.

Scrape the last of the lye from your bowl or cup with the spoon, then keep stirring till the lye is thoroughly dissolved. If you're using water or another transparent liquid, the solution will go from cloudy to clear, and in the end, you won't see any grains left in it. If the liquid is opaque, you can tell the lye is dissolved when your thermometer

Cool Technique

the lye solution. It makes no difference at all, especially if you're using a stick blender. A bit of trivia: This effect will most often be noticed with lower-fat milk.

Yet another effect produced by dissolving lye in milk is that the fat in the milk begins to saponify. If you're using cream, you will get a fairly stiff mixture at this point. Once again, you can find advice to the effect that the soap is worthless if this happens—and once again, it's just not so.

8. With milk, you're working with an opaque liquid, so there's no way to tell just by looking if the lye is dissolved. This is one of the main problems giving milk soap a reputation as difficult.

Luckily, there's a different way you can tell, as provided by one of the chemists helping me with this book. Once all the milk is melted, take the temperature of the mixture. At first, the temperature will seesaw or even rise. Stir the mixture a bit

Warm Technique

shows that the temperature of the solution has started to fall.

8. Once the lye is dissolved, you can cool the solution quickly with a water bath—but don't use the bath before then, because cooling will make the lye dissolve more slowly. Also, don't try the bath if your solution isn't in an unbreakable container like the stainless steel saucepan I recommend. A lye spill is one of those things you don't need.

Pour your cold or chilled water from the pitcher into the roasting pan or dishpan—not into the saucepan with the lye solution! Without floating the dishpan, make the surrounding water as deep as you can, then add ice cubes to it.

This bath will cool the lye solution most quickly if your saucepan is stainless steel instead of enameled. Stirring the solution will cool it even faster. And you'll see a *big* difference if you use a rack beneath the saucepan so the water can get under it.

Check the temperature of the lye

Cool Technique	**Warm Technique**

and keep checking. When the temperature definitely begins to fall, the lye is dissolved.

I found only one exception to this rule, and that's when you're making soap with high-fat liquids like cream. Because of the high proportion of fat, there's enough saponification that the temperature will continue to rise. In that case, just keep stirring for four or five minutes—that should be enough.

Not sure whether the amount of fat in your mixture will keep the temperature rising or let it fall? Here's an easy way to tell: If there's enough to keep the temperature rising, the mixture will also thicken noticeably as you stir. As long as it stays thin, you can count on a temperature drop to tell you the lye is dissolved.

solution, without letting the thermometer touch the bottom of the saucepan. You want it to get to about 115° F (46° C).

Combining the Ingredients

1. Take the saucepan of lye solution and your other lye utensils to your main work area.

Cool Technique	**Warm Technique**

Cool Technique

2. Take the melted fat and add it to the soup pot.

3. Pour your milk-and-lye solution through a sieve and into the soup pot with the fat. Or, if it's too thick to pour—as it will be with recipes that use high-fat milks—just spoon it into the pot.

4. Stir with the long-handled spoon until mixed. You may see an immediate thickening—it's probably the melted fat beginning to re-solidify from the cool temperature. The mixture will probably thin out again as you keep stirring.

Don't worry if the soap still has an ammonia-like smell. It will go away. But you should use good ventilation and avoid breathing the fumes.

Warm Technique

2. Check the temperature of your mixture of melted fat and milk. You want it to be quite warm—around 115° F (46° C). There's no need, though, to be overly particular about it. I've learned to judge by feel if my fat is warm enough—to me, this temperature feels "quite warm but not hot." (You might experiment sometime with heated water and a thermometer to get the feel of it.)

If necessary, re-warm the mixture in the microwave for a few seconds. (Just don't forget it in there!) Then pour the mixture into the soup pot with the liquid fat.

3. Pour the lye solution into the soup pot. The lye solution and the fat do NOT have to be at identical temperatures, but the final mixture should be somewhere around 115° F (46° C), and definitely not less than 100° F (38° C).

This really shouldn't be a problem—but if you ever find the temperature *is* below that minimum, you'll just have to proceed as is

Cool Technique	**Warm Technique**
	and hope for the best. You must *not* reheat any mixture with lye—that's asking for trouble!
	4. Stir briefly but well with the long-handled spoon to start mixing the ingredients. Don't worry if you smell a sharp, ammonia-like odor. It's normal, and it goes away. It's a by-product of the lye combining with the proteins in the milk. Although it isn't a problem for the soap, use good ventilation as you would for lye fumes, and avoid breathing the ammonia fumes.

5. Add any scent or liquid colorant and stir it in a bit.

6. With the thermometer, carefully check the temperature of your mixture and make a note of it. Again, it's best if the thermometer is waterproof, "instant-read," and digital.

7. Maintaining good ventilation, mix with the stick blender. Move it throughout the mixture so everything gets blended thoroughly, tipping the pot as you need to. While the stick blender is running, be careful to keep the blade submerged, or you'll stir air into the soap and may splash the mixture. Whenever you lift the blade out, take your finger off the button so the blade stops spinning before reaching the surface.

Keep blending the mixture, and you'll begin to see changes. Originally oily and transparent, it will become creamy and opaque. The surface, which was shiny at first, will become duller, and the oily ring at the edge of the mixture's surface—right where it meets the wall of the pot—will shrink and all but disappear.

Next you'll notice the mixture thickening and getting smoother. It will come to resemble thick eggnog or very thin pudding. At this point, you can stop blending, because the saponification that produces soap can continue without further mixing. You might call this "the point of no return."

Besides the visual signs, you can get a feel for the thickening by turning off the blender and briefly stirring with it like a spoon. With a weaker blender, you can even *hear* the difference, as the thickening slows down the blade, causing the sound of the motor to drop in pitch.

You should have little trouble recognizing the signs I've given—but if you're not sure, leave the stick blender off and hand-stir with it for about thirty seconds to see if the mixture thins out again. If it does, go back to blending. Again, good lighting makes a huge difference with the visual tests.

The final sign for you is temperature. When you notice the mixture growing thicker and smoother, start checking it again with your thermometer. Saponification generates heat, and when the mixture has reached "the point of no return," the temperature should have risen about a couple of degrees Fahrenheit (one degree Celsius).

Once it has, you're done. And you'll definitely want to stop by the time the temperature has risen five degrees Fahrenheit (three degrees Celsius). Just a few degrees above that, the mixture can suddenly become too thick to pour from the pot!

An experienced soapmaker can do without this temperature test, but I highly recommend it at least for your first few tries while you learn the other signs—especially if you're not working with a teacher. Beyond that, though, it's always a great final check. The one case I've found in which it doesn't work is with mixtures containing vegetable shortening. The temperature of these may not begin to rise till well after they've thickened enough.

Some special considerations:

Cool Technique	**Warm Technique**
With Cool Technique, you can get obvious thickening right away, most likely from the melted fat resolidifying as it blends with the cool lye solution. This is actually "false trace," and the way to deal with it is to stir with your spoon until the soap thins again. However, some soaps actually are ready to pour in a minute or two. The way to tell is with the thermometer. With false trace, you won't see a temperature rise.	You may sometimes need to blend for quite a while, depending on the recipe and the power of your stick blender. Don't count on it, though! Your soap may instead be ready to pour quite quickly.

8. Pour the mixture into your mold, scraping the pot with the rubber spatula. Don't cover the mold.

If your mold is flexible, remember to move it now only with the rack. Never move a flexible mold that's full of liquid soap unless it rests on a rack or other rigid support!

Cool Technique	Warm Technique
9. Put the mold in the refrigerator for at least three hours. Or if you want the palest possible color, first set it in the freezer for half an hour, then move it to the refrigerator. Just don't forget to take it out of the freezer! Later, when you take the mold from the refrigerator, you can set it on a counter or other location at room temperature.	9. Set the mold on a counter or other safe location at room temperature.

Cleanup

1. **Don't take off your gloves and goggles till you're finished cleaning up.**

2. If you use a dishwasher, wash your utensils once by hand before loading them. If you don't do this, your dishwasher will probably run over.

If you're washing *only* by hand, begin by squeezing a small amount of dish soap directly onto the surface to be washed—use no water at first. With a sponge, a cloth, or your gloved hand, work the dish soap into the oil or soap on the pot. Pay special attention to handles and the outer lip. Rinse well with hot water. This is the method for handwashing chemical lab ware, and it works as well as an automatic dishwasher.

3. Wipe down your work surfaces with a paper towel dampened with vinegar to neutralize traces of lye.

4. Wash your gloves *with your hands still inside them.*

5. *Now* take off your gloves and goggles.

Removal and Testing

Your soap should be solid in about twelve hours, and ready to come out of the mold and be tested in about twenty-four. At this point, the soap shouldn't be caustic, but you should work with your gloves on till you test it and you're sure.

Put a little distilled water on the surface of the soap, scrub a bit to make a paste, then push a pH strip into the paste. If the strip shows anything in the range of 7 to 10, the soap is fine. The exact pH reading doesn't matter—the strips don't measure all that accurately anyway. But they *will* let you know if your soap is in a safe range.

If the pH strip reads 11 or 12, let the soap sit for a few days and test it again. It may just need a little more time. If your reading is above 12, don't use the soap and don't even touch it without gloves. Sometimes a very high pH will slowly decrease till the soap is usable. More often, the soap should be discarded or rebatched. (For info on rebatching, see the FAQ in my book *Smart Soapmaking.*)

It's important to test for safety's sake, but don't let me scare you. If you follow the instructions in this book and use recipes that are properly designed, you should *never* see a pH reading that's dangerously high.

Cutting and Curing

After testing out successfully, your soap is ready to cut into bars. But cutting milk soap can be tricky. It may tend to chip, especially at the bottom of the cut. Sometimes, waiting another day will solve the problem. But sometimes it won't.

One simple solution is to turn your slab of soap on edge to cut it. Another is to use a large, sharp pizza-cutting wheel. Yet another, mostly for shorter cuts, is to use a cheese wire.

As you cut your soap, keep an eye on the cut surfaces. The texture should be fairly smooth and regular, with a consistency like cheese. It may be slightly sticky on the cut edges, and there may be a small difference in texture between the cut faces and the uncut ones—something like you'd see on a soft cheese with a rind. This is normal.

What you should *not* see is any lye granules. If you think maybe you see one, carefully wet the area with distilled water and lay a pH paper across the soap and the granule. If it's undissolved lye, it will "telegraph" as a dark spot against the paper's lighter background. If this happens, you have no choice but to discard or rebatch.

Even if the cut surfaces look good, still test at least one with the pH paper. If it tests OK, you're home free.

If you like, you can use a vegetable peeler or soap beveller to neaten the sides of the bars and bevel the edges.

Soap should dry out for a while, which also gives it a chance to grow milder. Set the bars somewhere with good air circulation, on a rack if possible. Curing time depends on how much liquid went into the soap, as well as on how it's stored and how humid the storage area. Minimum times normally range from a couple of weeks to a month, with the time for soaps from most of my recipes falling about halfway between, at three weeks. Soap with a very high percentage of liquid fat may need to dry even longer than a month.

How can you be sure the soap is dry enough? Just try a bar. If the lather is stringy or slimy, or if the soap gets used up too fast or gets gooey, that soap needs more time. The longer the bars dry—up to a couple of months or so—the harder they'll become and the longer they'll last in use.

More Recipes!
Different Milk Soaps You Can Try

On the following pages are more recipes to use with the Cool and Warm techniques. Just follow the directions I've already given for those, unless a recipe says otherwise. All my recipes use 30 oz of fat (850 g).

If you want to add scent, start with the manufacturer's directions for amount, or use about 1.2 oz (about 35 g)—but before choosing one, read about possible unwanted effects in my later chapter on controlling color. See that chapter too before using any colorant—you're not likely to get what you expect!

Adapting Between Cool and Warm

If you want to use a Cool Technique recipe with powdered milk instead of fluid—or use a Warm Technique recipe with fluid milk instead of powdered—the recipes are easy to adapt.

To use powdered milk in a Cool Technique recipe, just reconstitute the powder with water, using the proportions and instructions on the package. Unless those instructions specify that cool water will work, use warm or even hot—and remember, for soapmaking the water must be *distilled*. If you have no instructions, reconstitute at the ratio of 1 oz milk powder to 8 oz water (28 g milk powder to 227 g water). Once the milk is in fluid form, follow my directions for Cool Technique.

To use fluid milk in a Warm Technique recipe, substitute milk directly for the water called for—in other words, leave out the water in the recipe and add an equal amount of milk. Freeze the milk and, again, proceed with my instructions for *Cool* Technique.

It may seem illogical at first that, either way you adapt, you're going to use Cool Technique. But remember, Warm Technique is only for milk *powder*. Whether you adapt from Cool to Warm, or from Warm to Cool, you wind up using fluid milk—so Cool Technique is what you need.

Recipe Checking

Before you try a new soap recipe—mine or anyone else's—always check the given lye and water amounts to make sure they're correct. Don't use the recipe till you're sure it has no errors, even if it comes from a published book—and that goes double for any recipe you find on the Internet.

Though you can do the math yourself, the simplest and safest way to check a recipe is with a *lye calculator*. These tell you how much lye and water you should use for a given quantity of fat. Many such calculators can be found and used on the Web for free—just search on "lye calculator"—and they're found in some computer programs as well.

Lye calculators don't require you to do any math—just enter the amount of each fat. The calculator then gives you the correct amounts of lye and liquid to use. Some also give information about the properties of the soap you'll get.

Yogurt Parfait Soap
(Cool Technique)

Parfait means "perfect," and that's the way this recipe turned out. It's really just a variation on the basic recipe, but my recipe testers liked it so much, I decided to feature it. During the testing, I kept getting emails: "Soap 20 was great!" "I like everything about this one!" "What in the world is in Soap 20? It's the best of all!" No one guessed it didn't have any luxury ingredients in it.

I still think of it as "Soap 20," but I guess "Yogurt Parfait" sounds more interesting.

First combine the water and yogurt thoroughly with a whisk, making sure there are no lumps. Then freeze, and proceed with the instructions for Cool Technique.

> 9 oz (255 g) coconut oil
> 21 oz (595 g) olive oil
> 4.5 oz (128 g) distilled water
> 4.5 oz (128 g) whole milk yogurt
> 4.1 oz (116 g) lye

Apricot Cream Soap
(Cool Technique)

This soap is made with whipping cream. For soapmaking, I prefer it at the lighter end of its normal fat range—about 30%. If your cream is much heavier than that, you can dilute it with milk.

When the lye melts the frozen cream, the mixture will be very thick, like mashed potatoes. Because of the high fat content, you won't be able to use temperature as a guide to whether the lye is dissolved—so stir, stir, and stir some more. It may take five minutes. And don't use flake lye here. It won't dissolve properly.

I tried adding a small amount of pureed apricots to this recipe. My advice is: Save the apricots to eat. They reduced the lather of my soap quite noticeably and made it feel rough.

3.4 oz (96 g) shea butter
10 oz (283 g) coconut oil
10 oz (283 g) apricot kernel oil
4.4 oz (125 g) olive oil
2.2 oz (62 g) castor oil
9 oz (255 g) whipping cream, about 30% fat
4.1 oz (116 g) lye

Milk White Soap
(Cool Technique)

This is the palest milk soap I could come up with. For an almost paper-white soap, use coconut milk. Soaps with dairy milks often take on a faint creamy tinge with time, even if they're perfectly white when new.

This recipe calls for Crisco, a popular American brand of vegetable shortening. In other parts of the world, you can safely substitute any other shortening made of soy and cottonseed oils alone.

> 10 oz (283 g) coconut oil
> 4 oz (113 g) Crisco
> 2 oz (57 g) castor oil
> 6 oz (170 g) sunflower oil
> 8 oz (227 g) almond oil
> 9 oz (255 g) fluid milk
> 4.2 oz (119 g) lye

Buttermilk Castile Soap
(Cool Technique)

Because of the buttermilk, this isn't a purist's Castile soap. But it's a great soap anyway.

That is, *if* you let it age for two to three months. The first time I made this soap, I tried it right away and disliked the lather so much, I threw away most of the batch. Much later, I happened to use the lone surviving bar and loved it. Hard but lathery, scented with rosemary essential oil, that bar got used to the last sliver.

> 30 oz (850 g) olive oil
> 9 oz (255 g) buttermilk
> 3.8 oz (108 g) lye

Cinnamon Oatmeal Soap
(Cool Technique)

I almost never suggest a specific scent for a soap, but this one is very nice with a good oatmeal-milk-and-honey scent. I also almost never give volume measurements in a soap recipe. But there's no need for precision with the oatmeal and cinnamon.

If you can't buy half-and-half, produce your own by mixing equal portions of light or single cream and milk.

10.5 oz (298 g) coconut oil
1.2 oz (34 g) shea butter
6.6 oz (187 g) sunflower oil
11.7 oz (332 g) olive oil
1 tsp cinnamon
1 tbsp finely-chopped oatmeal
9 oz (255 g) half-and-half
4.2 oz (119 g) lye

Sour Cream Soap
(Cool Technique)

This is a grocery-store soap, one you can make from readily available ingredients. It's also excellent—very good lather and moisturizing. And it's very pale, almost paper-white.

First combine the water and sour cream thoroughly with a whisk, making sure there are no lumps. Then freeze, and proceed with the instructions for Cool Technique.

If the soap thickens right after you add the sour-cream-and-lye mixture to the fat, hand stir a little till it becomes thinner. Then stick blend, repeating the hand stirring if the mixture again thickens too soon. When the soap really is ready to pour, it will be even-textured and not shiny or pearly-looking.

This recipe calls for Crisco, a popular American brand of vegetable shortening. In other parts of the world, you can safely substitute any other shortening made of soy and cottonseed oils alone.

> 10 oz (283 g) coconut oil
> 10 oz (283 g) Crisco
> 10 oz (283 g) olive oil
> 4.5 oz (128 g) sour cream
> 4.5 oz (128 g) distilled water
> 4.2 oz (119 g) lye

Deena's Avocado Cream Soap
(Cool Technique)

My friend Deena sent me a bar of soap that was absolute perfection. I was hesitant to ask her about it—why would she share the secret of such a wonderful recipe?

Finally, I got up my nerve and emailed to ask what fats were in it. When I got her reply, I had to laugh. Turned out, she'd used one of *my* recipes from *Smart Soapmaking,* substituting cream for water.

Deena used cream from her goats, but cow cream works too. Either way, this is one of my favorite soaps.

If your whipping cream is much heavier than the 30% fat I recommend, you can dilute it with milk.

> 2.5 oz (71 g) avocado butter
> 7.5 oz (213 g) coconut oil
> 12.5 oz (354 g) avocado oil
> 7.5 oz (213 g) olive oil
> 9 oz (255 g) whipping cream, about 30% fat
> 4.1 oz (116 g) lye

Marge's Chocolate Silk Soap
(Cool Technique)

This recipe is a gift from my friend Marge—chocolate lover and soap designer par excellence. There are three variations: Milk Chocolate, Dark Chocolate, and White Chocolate. All three have a lush, silky lather.

Marge doesn't scent these. I use chocolate fragrance oil in the Milk or Dark Chocolate versions, but not in the White Chocolate one.

Hand stir instead of stick blending. This soap saponifies very quickly.

> 7.5 oz (213 g) finely-grated unrefined cocoa butter
> 7.5 oz (213 g) coconut oil
> 13.1 oz (371 g) shea oil
> 1.9 oz (54 g) castor oil
> 5 oz (142 g) whole milk
> 4.0 oz (113 g) lye
> Plus ingredients for one of the variations below

Milk Chocolate Variation: Add 5 oz (142 g) chocolate milk.

Dark Chocolate Variation: Add 5 oz (142 g) chocolate milk and 1 tsp unsweetened cocoa powder. Mix the cocoa powder with a little of the shea oil, and mix this into the rest of the fat.

White Chocolate Variation: Use an additional 5 oz (142 g) whole milk and 1 oz (28 g) white chocolate chips. Melt the chocolate chips with the rest of the solid fat.

Milly's Milk Soap
(Cool Technique)

Milly says, "I chose most of the ingredients for their skin benefits. The olive is excellent for all skin types, especially sensitive skins; the coconut gives the lather we all love to see in the shower; the apricot kernel and rice bran have excellent skin-nourishing properties; and cocoa butter makes the soap longer-lasting. The goat milk gives it a luxury feel and is excellent for those with sensitive or problem skins."

> 9 oz (255 g) coconut oil
> 3.9 oz (111 g) finely-grated cocoa butter
> 12 oz (340 g) olive oil
> 2.5 oz (71 g) rice bran oil
> 2.6 oz (74 g) apricot kernel oil
> 9 oz (255 g) goat milk
> 4.2 oz (119 g) lye

AHA! Buttermilk Soap
(Warm Technique)

AHA stands for alpha hydroxy acid, a much-touted beauty treatment. Fermented milks contain AHAs. Legend tells us that Cleopatra bathed in milk—if so, she must have known all about them. I'm not at all sure that any AHAs survive the soapmaking process, but this is a very nice soap regardless.

Hemp oil has a scent of its own, a slightly hay-like fragrance. It fades but doesn't disappear completely. That scent is nice by itself if you want to leave it like that, or you can try adding herbal or woody scents. Another thing about hemp oil is that it tends to be green to gold in color. So, this recipe isn't a good choice if you're looking for white soap.

You may notice that this recipe calls for more lye than most. Just to reassure you: It's not a misprint. (But you're going to check it anyway, right? Never fail to check a recipe, I don't care who gave it to you. Even me.)

> 9 oz (255 g) coconut oil
> 7 oz (198 g) aloe vera butter
> 8 oz (227 g) hemp oil
> 6 oz (170 g) olive oil
> 1 oz (28 g) buttermilk powder
> 9 oz (255 g) distilled water
> 4.5 oz (128 g) lye

Milk-and-Honey Facial Soap
(Warm Technique)

Aloe vera liquid replaces water in this soap. Its color will be on the golden side, caused by the reaction between honey and lye, which occurs regardless of temperature.

Combine the honey with the milk powder before blending the powder into the melted fat. Otherwise, it's made just like any other Warm Technique recipe.

As with any soap, let this mellow for several weeks before using it on your face.

> 5 oz (142 g) shea butter
> 8 oz (227 g) coconut oil
> 7 oz (198 g) almond oil
> 7 oz (198 g) hazelnut oil
> 3 oz (85 g) olive oil
> 1 oz (28 g) powdered milk
> 9 oz (255 g) aloe vera liquid
> 0.3 oz (9 g) honey
> 4.1 oz (116 g) lye

Non-Veggie Milk Soap
(Warm Technique)

This is a hard soap, with good lather and cleansing. It's also fairly pale-colored.

Home-rendered lard may have an odor, but the grocery-store kind has little or none, so I'd recommend that instead.

> 9.7 oz (275 g) lard
> 9.8 oz (278 g) coconut oil
> 10 oz (283 g) sweet almond oil
> 0.5 oz (14 g) castor oil
> 1 oz (28 g) powdered milk
> 9 oz (255 g) distilled water
> 4.2 oz (119 g) lye

Longer-Lasting Milk Soap
(Warm Technique)

This recipe produces a hard soap that will last. It has good lather, but it's not particularly moisturizing, so I like to use it for hand soap. It does well in decorative molds.

13 oz (369 g) coconut oil
2 oz (57 g) shea butter
2 oz (57 g) finely-grated cocoa butter
13 oz (369 g) olive oil
1 oz (28 g) powdered milk
8 oz (227 g) distilled water
4.4 oz (125 g) lye

Laurie's Silk and Milk Soap
(Warm Technique)

Silk fibers in soap add a special touch. Dissolved completely, they give it a unique smoothness. This is also a good soap for fancy molds, because the beeswax makes the shapes hold well.

With sharp scissors, cut the silk fibers into pieces of about half an inch (about a centimeter). Put them into your empty saucepan before adding the water. Let the fibers soak for half an hour. When you add the lye, stir constantly to keep the silk fibers moving, and keep stirring after the lye is dissolved till the fibers are too. For this one, don't use a slotted spoon—the fibers will get tangled together in the slots and not dissolve.

This recipe needs warmer temperatures than others because of the beeswax, so combine your milk-and-fat mixture and your lye solution at 125°–150° F (52°–66° C). Stir and then stick blend lightly—the soap often saponifies in a short time.

> 8 oz (227 g) coconut oil
> 6 oz (170 g) shea butter
> 2 oz (57 g) beeswax granules
> 12 oz (340 g) olive oil
> 4 oz (113 g) safflower oil (preferably high oleic)
> Silk fibers, a wad about the size of a pecan in the shell
> 1.2 oz (34 g) powdered milk
> 10.5 oz (298 g) distilled water
> 4.3 oz (122 g) lye

Ruth's Butter Soap
(Warm Technique)

This recipe lets you get the benefits of butterfat in your soap without dealing with milk. The butter can be either cow or goat.

To melt the solid fat, you can microwave for a minute, then remove, stir, and repeat as needed. Or melt it, as Ruth does, in a slow cooker set on low. The slow cooker takes longer but is easier.

The fat will not be completely transparent when melted because of the milk solids in the butter.

> 4 oz (113 g) coconut oil
> 9 oz (255 g) finely-grated cocoa butter
> 4 oz (113 g) unsalted butter (cow or goat)
> 10 oz (283 g) olive oil
> 3 oz (85 g) castor oil
> 9 oz (255 g) distilled water
> 4 oz (113 g) lye

Making Soap with Plant Milks
Vegans Do It Too!

Don't want to use animal milks? Not to worry. The plant world offers plenty of milks for making soap.

Soapmakers who often use plant milks may choose to make their own. You can find recipes for plant milks on the Internet by using keywords such as "make almond milk" (or whatever kind you want). Select a recipe without sugary additives like dates.

For experimenting and trying new things, though, you may want to start with purchased plant milks. Commonly available ones include soy, coconut, rice, and almond.

It's important to remember that coconut milk is the only one of the four that is reasonably standardized. In commercial form, soy, rice, and almond milk are proprietary products, and their composition varies. The manufacturers aren't, after all, in the business of making good soapmaking liquids—they're trying to offer palatable beverages. The ingredients are on the labels, of course, but the actual formulas are secret, with major differences between brands. And even the same company may sell different varieties and versions.

So, here are the results of my experiments, along with the warning that your results might not be the same with every product from every company.

I found soy and coconut milks to be easiest to use. They made good soap no matter what I did. As with dairy milks, using them with Cool Technique minimizes discoloration. You can substitute them for dairy milk in any Cool Technique recipe.

When you freeze soy milk, and again when you combine it with lye, it may discolor temporarily. As you proceed with your soapmaking, the color becomes much lighter. My finished soy milk soap was beige. In my tests, I used Silk Soymilk, "Plain."

I tried several brands of full-fat, unsweetened canned coconut milk. I also tried infusing coconut milk myself from fresh coconut. That was an interesting experiment, but the soap wasn't as good, so I recommend the canned. With Cool Technique, the coconut milk remained quite pale, as did the final soap. (I also got a fairly pale, cream-colored soap just with the standard method from my book *Smart Soapmaking*.)

Almond and rice milk presented more of a challenge, possibly because they're solutions with fairly large particles. When I used Cool Technique with almond milk, I had a total failure. A powdery crust rose to the top as the mixture set in the mold, very similar to the results I'd gotten at first with milk powders.

That inspired me to try another batch, this time with a variation of Warm Technique. It worked perfectly. So, you can use any Warm Technique recipe with almond milk, substituting it in equal weight for the water in the recipe. Just ignore the step of blending the powdered milk into the fat.

The almond milk I used was Blue Diamond Almond Breeze, "Original." The soap turned out a very pale yellow.

With rice milk, I never did get satisfactory soap. My batches developed a heavy powdery surface with Cool Technique, a light one with Warm. I used Rice Dream, "Original." I've since heard of other soapmakers having better luck with rice milk made at home, but I haven't tried that myself. So, at least for now, I can't recommend rice milk for soapmaking.

Other vegan milk substitutes include hemp, hazelnut, oat, and multigrain. When deciding how to work with one of them, it may help to consider which of the plant milks that I've tested are most similar to the one you have in mind. Don't forget, though—when you use untested products or methods, your efforts may or may not produce good soap. On the other hand, the one thing you're certain to get is information.

There are also a few things to keep in mind when choosing among brands and varieties of a particular plant milk. If vanilla has been added, it will probably discolor the soap. If there's added sugar, you'll have to be careful it doesn't scorch when you add the lye.

One final recommendation: With all plant milks in Cool Technique—even more so than with animal milks—you should strain the milk-and-lye solution through a sieve when adding it to the fat. Small, solid particles may be produced by the lye's reaction with the milk. They might well be broken up when you stick blend, but strain the solution first anyway to be sure.

Getting Your Milk Soap in Shape
How to Choose and Use a Mold

Soap molds can be almost any shape, size, or material—but for milk soapmaking, avoid molds that let heat build up in the soap. Otherwise, the milk sugars will caramelize, turning the milk brown and possibly reducing the lather.

For the recipes in this book, you'll need a mold—or group of molds—holding a volume of 5 cups (1.2 l).

Kinds of Mold

Tray molds are large, shallow boxes, one bar in depth. They're very well suited to milk soaps. To limit heat, it's important that the soap be in a sheet no deeper than about an inch (about two-and-a-half centimeters).

Given that depth, you can quickly calculate whether a square or rectangular tray mold is the right size for my recipes. Just figure the area of the bottom by multiplying the length times the width. You want it to come out somewhere near 64 square inches (near 400 square centimeters).

Tray molds may include ornamental patterns, as well as raised lines that make grooves in the soap to guide your cutting it into individual bars. Or they may have dividers you can insert to form individual bars after pouring in your soap mixture.

Baking pans can be used as tray molds—just don't use aluminum, since it reacts with lye. You can even use a shallow cardboard box, if it's sturdy.

Individual bar molds work very well for milk soaps. Craft stores sell these for working with melt-and-pour soap. Or use "snack size" disposable/reusable food storage containers. The ones I buy have a maximum capacity of about a cup and a half (about one-third liter), though you won't fill them completely. They make a large, easy-to-hold bar with an attractive raised border.

There are also crosses between tray molds and individual bar molds—trays made of a series of separate molds for individual bars. These are commonly used for ornamented soaps.

Block or *loaf* or *log molds* make a thick block of soap. These work well for water-based soaps, and for that reason I featured them in my book *Smart Soapmaking*. But they do *not* work well for most milk soaps, because soap in that shape retains and concentrates heat, causing the milk to darken. Still, you might use such a mold with fermented milks like buttermilk, which are less affected by heat.

Various other household objects can be used for soap molds. Keep in mind that the object's shape must allow the soap to be removed easily. It's best if the mold is a little wider at top than at bottom.

Whether you buy your soap mold or find something around your home, milk soapmaking requires that it be made from material that doesn't trap heat. Wood and glass don't work well. Thin metal is good, but remember not to use aluminum. Plastic works well, especially if you grease it lightly with petroleum jelly or mineral oil. (*Lightly* is the key word here. You don't want an oil slick on your soap.)

My experiences with silicone baking pans have not been good. All worked beautifully for a few batches, but after that, they began to break down. One leaked color into a batch of soap. Another merged with the soap where they touched to make something like bathtub caulk. Both batches had to be thrown away—along with the pans, of course.

"Silicone" is actually not a single substance but a group of synthetic compounds. It seems that some of these compounds work well for soap and others don't. Silicone molds from a reputable vendor of soap supplies *should* be satisfactory, but you'll have to find out for yourself. And if you buy silicone pans sold just for food, you're taking a bigger chance.

If you do use a mold from silicone or another flexible material, support it on a metal rack when in use—a cake cooling rack or something similar—and lift them together by the rack until the soap is solid. You can't directly pick up a flexible mold full of liquid soap without considerable danger of spilling. I use a wire mesh "in-basket" from an office supply store. It's perfect, because the raised sides hold the mold securely and the open mesh lets the heat escape.

Whatever kind of mold you use, be careful to set it perfectly level. Even a tiny tilt is enough to make the soap crooked, and that's much less appealing.

Lining a Soap Mold (or Not)

To be sure you can remove your soap, place a lining inside any rigid mold that can't be taken apart or destroyed. Molds made of absorbent materials like cardboard also must be lined. As with so much in soapmaking, the need for lining may depend on the recipe. A high percentage of liquid fat makes your soap more likely to stick.

Good lining materials include:

• Pieces of plastic tarp

• Freezer paper (with the shiny side toward the soap)
• Plastic bags that fit your mold (with any printing on the side away from the soap)
• Parchment paper
• Plastic wrap

DO NOT USE ALUMINUM FOIL. Again, aluminum reacts with lye. If you use a tray mold that isn't flared at the top, line it with something strong enough not to tear when you tug on it.

A square or rectangular mold can be lined safely with one sheet of paper folded at the corners, or with one piece of flexible plastic. Make sure it's big enough to cover the bottom and all sides, with at least a bit sticking up at the top.

Another simple kind of liner is two overlapping rectangles. For instance, you can use two pieces of plastic tarp—one rectangle laid into the mold lengthwise, another crosswise. Each piece should be long enough to cover the bottom and two sides, again with a little bit sticking over.

With plastic linings, the heavier the plastic, the fewer the wrinkles in the surface of your soap. The trash bags meant for outdoor garbage cans will work better than the smaller, thinner-walled bags for kitchen trash.

Plastic and paper liners can be made to fit tightly if the mold is first greased with shortening. Press the liner against the greased surface, which acts as a temporary glue.

If you don't want to use a liner, there are several tricks you can try. Some molds will release the soap if you place them, soap and all, in the freezer for about an hour. Be warned: Sometimes this works and sometimes it doesn't. Another trick with a tray mold is to cut the soap into bars before removing it. You may have to sacrifice one bar, but you can then get underneath the others.

Since petroleum jelly and mineral oil will not saponify, some soapmakers use them to grease molds, much as a cook would use shortening to grease a cake pan. Others don't like the residue those products leave on the soap.

Using Decorative Molds

Particularly for pale soaps, molds with intricate surface patterns are popular and produce an attractive bar. Such patterns include raised or incised floral motifs, Celtic knots, text, pictures of animals, and many other decorations.

Some shapes and patterns allow easier soap removal than others. The deeper, finer, or more intricate the pattern, the more likely that removing the soap will be a problem. With harder soaps, fine patterns may require greasing with mineral oil. Be careful not to use so much oil that it fills the pattern.

With softer soaps, molds with delicate or fine patterns may not work well at all. Even if you give the soap plenty of curing time in the mold, you may later see the pattern in the soap lose crispness.

With Cool Technique soaps, it's a bit of a balancing act to get the soap to set hard enough to take the mold's pattern properly while still keeping the soap from darkening. Here's the way I worked out with no additives:

As soon as you pour the soap into the molds, put them in the freezer, making sure they're level. Leave them there for half an hour. Then remove the molds from the freezer and put them in the refrigerator for another 24 hours. For all of this, leave the soap in the molds. It will seem quite hard when it comes out of the freezer, but that's only because it's so cold—it still can't hold a shape on its own.

When the soap comes out of the refrigerator, set it somewhere at room temperature—still in the molds—for another 48 hours. At this point, the soap should be firm enough to take out of the molds, but test it first with a fingertip to be sure. If the soap is hard enough to resist denting, it's firm enough to remove. If it's still soft, leave it alone for a while longer.

Once it's firm enough, gently flex the molds and see if the soap pops out. If it doesn't, don't force it—it won't come out cleanly. Return the molds to the freezer for a couple of hours—that almost always works.

With Warm Technique, soap shouldn't be chilled until after it's hardened. All the batches I chilled right after pouring developed a heavy coating of greasy powder on top. But Warm Technique soap may be chilled in a refrigerator or freezer *after* it's hardened, to help free it from the molds. Once cold, the soap usually comes out quickly and cleanly.

Controlling Your Color
How to Keep It Light

Soapmakers may expect milk soaps to be white—and white soaps do a beautiful job of showing off intricate patterns in decorative molds. But it's not always easy to get very pale colors in milk soaps. Even if your soap is pure white when it comes out of the mold, it may darken slightly as it cures.

I've discussed some of this as we've gone along, but here are the factors you deal with in managing color.

Color of the milk. Milk isn't pure white. It varies from pale to darker creamy tones. Unless you use pigment to lighten your soap, it can't be a lighter color than the milk it's made from.

Evaporated milk is concentrated and partly caramelized from the canning process, so it's the darkest. Cream has a yellowish cast because of its high fat content. With careful handling, coconut milk may stay very pale.

Color of the fats. Many fats add color to milk soap, while some don't, and this is one of the most important factors. Lard, vegetable shortening, sunflower oil, and coconut oil are among the fats that add no color.

Sometimes a different version of a fat can be used to minimize or eliminate color effects. For example, most olive oils are more or less green, but their colors still vary widely. The "extra light" culinary olive oils make a lighter-colored soap than most others. Some "Refined A" olive oil is colorless and can be used in white soaps.

Refined shea butter may also work for white soap, while raw or unrefined shea butter will give a yellowish cast.

Temperature. The unwanted effects of heat on milk soaps are the main reason for using my Cool Technique. Milk contains sugars that begin to caramelize and turn brown at about 160° F (71° C). This affects both color and lather. Fermented milks like buttermilk have less sugar, but some is still present.

For palest color, some milk soaps should be refrigerated after pouring into the molds—though in general, soaps made with milk powder won't tolerate this.

Reaction to lye. Even if you're careful to keep the temperature of your mixture low, some milks will discolor when mixed with lye. They may turn yellow, orangish, or brownish. Don't give up if you see this! The discoloring will probably disappear as you proceed.

Some fats have pronounced color in the bottle but lighten considerably as they saponify. In one test, I used a hemp oil that was almost emerald green—but the soap turned out a pale beige.

Type of mold. Molds should be made of materials that lose heat quickly, such as metal or thin plastic. Wood and glass tend to hold heat and cause the soap to discolor.

The shape of the mold influences both heat retention and concentration. If you use a block mold, even if you chill it, you'll have a darker center where the soap has become hotter during saponification. The best mold choices for pale-colored milk soaps are tray molds and individual bar molds. For best color control, fill them no deeper than an inch (two-and-a-half centimeters).

Fermented milks don't have to be handled quite as carefully. I've poured these into a wood block mold without getting the characteristic dark center. The soap was a light tan—probably a bit darker than if I'd used a tray mold, but even-colored throughout.

Scents. Vendors usually list a few fragrance oils as discoloring. The best known of these is vanilla, which will color the soap a dark brown. However, *many* fragrance oils contain a *little* vanilla—enough to turn the soap beige—and these are often *not* identified as discoloring. If you want the palest possible soap while using fragrance oils, you'll have to either ask your vendor about individual ones or experiment with them—or possibly both.

Strongly discoloring fragrance oils, such as vanilla or chocolate, may behave unpredictably in milk soaps, especially with Warm Technique. The problem is worse with fragrance oils that accelerate trace or cause the soap to heat. You may get uneven discoloring—either a random marbling or a darkened center. Sometimes these markings fade and blend in as the overall color darkens—and sometimes they don't.

If you're using a discoloring fragrance oil, be very careful to work within the specified temperature ranges. Also, you may get better results if you pour into individual bar molds, since they're less likely to build up heat. If a fragrance oil gives you trouble in a Warm Technique recipe despite all reasonable precautions, reconstitute the milk and use Cool Technique.

Fragrance oils may also cause a temporary overall color change—I've especially noticed a tendency to turn soap various shades of red or pink. This is likely to change to brown or beige in a week or so, so don't panic right away if it's ugly.

Most essential oils don't alter the soap color. But since a few do, you may have to ask questions and experiment with these as well.

Among the essential oils that may discolor your soap are citrus oils, patchouli, German chamomile, and those with a strong color of their own. On the other hand, lavender and rosemary essential oils have never changed a soap's color in my experiments—so if you want a neutral essential oil, these are ones I'd recommend.

Colorants. Soapmakers will tell you that the effects of colorants in milk soap are unpredictable. This is *not* a myth. Even if you start with a soap that's very white, the colorant may not do what you expect.

If using a colorant is important to you, work with a vendor who has good customer service and follow their recommendations for type and amount. Even so, be prepared to sacrifice a batch or two in the cause of experiment. The color may darken, lighten, or shift in hue as the soap saponifies.

Color swirls in soap are lovely, but they're likely to take considerable experimenting. I've seen some odd color combinations with swirled milk soaps. Several factors come into play here: the color of the base soap, the way the colorant reacts with the mixture, and how the two colors look together once the soap is cured.

Also, I find swirling much easier with a block mold than with a tray—and, of course, block molds aren't a good choice for most milk soaps. But if you want to do swirls in milk soaps, by all means give it a try—besides the odd ones I've seen, there have been some lovely ones.

Why, Why, Why?
Frequently Asked Questions

How do I substitute other ingredients for the ones in your recipes?

You can substitute one kind of fluid milk for another, or one kind of powdered milk for another. But don't substitute fats in my recipes or in *any* soap recipe—construct a new recipe, and check it with a lye calculator. Instructions for doing this are in my book *Smart Soapmaking*.

What are the advantages of using fluid milk and the Cool Technique? What are the disadvantages?

You may prefer soap made with fluid milk—some of my testers did. If you milk your own goats or other dairy livestock, Cool Technique will be your natural choice. If you want to use cream as your liquid, Cool Technique is the only choice, since cream isn't easily available in powdered form. In addition, you'll find that Cool Technique produces much less lye fumes.

Disadvantages are having to pre-freeze the milk, the increased risk of "false trace," and needing to use a form of lye that will dissolve easily in cool liquid.

What are the advantages of using powdered milk and the Warm Technique? What are the disadvantages?

Except for using a slightly higher temperature, Warm Technique is very similar to ordinary cold process soapmaking. You're much less likely to have problems with "false trace" if you use Warm Technique. It makes it easier to do special effects like color swirls.

Another advantage is that teas, aloe vera juice, or other liquids can be used without reducing the milk content of the soap. Flake lye can be used with Warm Technique—and that's less likely than bead lye to fly around or make you cough.

The big disadvantage of Warm Technique is that not all milk products are available in powdered form. Also, the lye solution emits more fumes. And you have to wait for that solution to cool before you can add it to the fat.

Finally, the poured soap can't be chilled in the mold to reduce darkening of the milk due to heat. When I chilled soaps made by Warm Technique, a coating of milk powder rose to the top. On the other hand, Warm Technique soaps tend to darken less, so the soaps are about the same color as Cool Technique soaps anyway.

Why do I have to freeze the milk for Cool Technique? I don't care if the soap is light-colored.

I think it's best to freeze the milk anyway. Milk sugar contributes to lathering, and it's caramelized or even burned from the heat of the dissolving lye unless the milk is frozen.

On the other hand, as long as you use tray molds, it's up to you whether to refrigerate the soap in the mold after pouring. The soap will be paler if you do, but that's the only effect I noted.

In Warm Technique, do I really need to mix the powdered milk with the melted fat? I've heard I can just add the powder at the end.

I've heard that too, and I tested it—along with similar procedures, as I tried to simplify Warm Technique. For all I know, it could work with some recipes—maybe ones with less powdered milk than I use. But each attempted "simplification" ended up with some of the powder not properly worked in. Results varied from a thick greasy crust on top of the soap to a subtle gritty feeling when I used it. I never got a soap that satisfied me without blending the powder into the melted fat.

Your instructions are for a microwave oven, but what if I don't have one?

You can melt the solid fat in a slow cooker, or in a regular oven at the lowest possible heat. It does take longer.

I don't recommend melting fat on a stovetop. Not that you *can't* do it, and do it safely. But there are a lot of "if's"—*if* you use a double boiler, *if* you pay close and constant attention, *if* you're prepared to handle a grease fire if one starts. I don't do it, and again, I don't recommend it.

Why do you use a stainless steel saucepan for mixing the lye solution? Everyone else says to use a glass measuring cup. Also, why do I need the roasting pan of tap water?

With all the temperature changes involved with milk soaps, I prefer metal to glass. Even oven-safe glass can crack or break if subjected to quick temperature changes.

The roasting pan of tap water speeds up the boring process of waiting for your lye to cool.

Why is it so important to add the lye to the water instead of the other way around? I've seen sources that say you can add water to lye.

One or two books and a few Web sites say to add water to lye. DON'T DO IT. Adding water to lye is dangerous, because the reaction is so strong. The U.S. Consumer Product Safety Commission actually recalled one soapmaking book for giving this advice. We're also warned not to add lye to warm or hot water, again because of the strong reaction.

Why do you say to avoid breathing the ammonia odor you get when lye combines with milk?

Though these fumes aren't as unpleasant as the ones you get from lye, some people are more sensitive to them than others. I'm one. I've found that, if I'm not careful, I'll have a mild sore throat after making several batches of milk soap in a day. Other soapmakers have told me it's not a problem for them.

My own solution is to cover my stovetop with a commercial-size cookie sheet and make the soap right under the range hood with the fan running. That doesn't take care of it entirely, but it helps.

Why don't you teach about trace like all the other soapmaking books?

Soapmakers use the word *trace* to describe the point at which a soap mixture is ready to pour into the mold. As a novice, I found the idea of trace to be the most intimidating thing about soapmaking. How in the world would I be able to figure it out? None of the photos or explanations in soapmaking books enlightened me.

Once someone actually showed it to me, I got it. But even after making soap for years, I'm not especially fond of the concept.

The name comes from the "trace" of soap mixture that stands out a little above the surface if you pour a trail of the mixture from a spoon back into the pot. At the point you observe that, soap is ready to pour for sure. But I'd say it's *more* than ready. In many cases, you get better texture in your soap by pouring sooner.

What's more, beginners often keep blending beyond that, not stopping till they get very heavy trace, because they're unsure whether they've reached the right point. Increasing their uncertainty is that they've probably heard of "false trace" and want to avoid it, but they may not know what it is or what causes it.

Actually, when soap is *first* ready to pour, you *can* observe a "trace-like" sign of it. Trailing the soap across the surface, you get a thin, hair-like, or scar-like darkening along the trail. This is *before* you'd get the raised path called trace, and it means you've mixed enough. But it's just one sign among many, and not the easiest to see, since it's visible only in *very* good light.

When I wrote *Smart Soapmaking,* I broke with tradition and emphasized methods other than observing trace for telling when soap is ready. I think this is one reason the book has gained the reputation of being the best one today for beginners.

What is false trace? I read about that, and now I'm not sure if my soap is ready to pour, or if it's just false trace.

"False trace" is when your soap mixture thickens considerably but then re-separates into lye solution and fat. It's rare in regular soapmaking, but it can happen when the temperature of your mixture falls below the recommended range, causing melted fat to resolidify. The thickening can fool you into thinking the mixture has saponified when it really hasn't.

With hand stirring, this cooling and thickening might happen anytime, but with stick blending, you would probably only see it right after you start. You'll know it's too early for saponification to have more than barely begun, and in any case, the mixture will show no significant temperature rise when measured with a thermometer. So, just keep blending, and the mixture should appear normal in a minute or so.

You're most likely to see this in milk soapmaking if you're using Cool Technique with a recipe that has a high proportion of solid fat. Again, checking for a temperature rise will keep you from mistaking false trace for genuine readiness to pour. Another thing that's helpful is if you know your recipe. Know if you have a scent or other ingredient that can cause the mixture to saponify rapidly. If you do, early thickening is something you probably need to act on. If you don't have one, and if your recipe has a lot of solid fat, you probably should wait and see.

I've noticed that milk soaps in false trace have a pearly look, like some shampoos. If your soap thickens and looks shiny and pearly right after you add the lye solution to the fat, hand stir a bit until it thins out again.

Can I hand stir milk soap instead of stick blending?

I wouldn't, as a rule. Aside from how much longer the hand stirring would take, some of the products of lye, milk protein, and milk fat may give your soap an unappealing texture if you don't break them up by stick blending. But you might switch between the two, particularly with recipes that are quick to saponify. And occasionally you'll find one so quick that you may want to *only* hand stir.

Help! My soap still smells like ammonia!

The ammonia smell you get when lye reacts with protein may go away by the time the soap has hardened, or it may linger a bit longer. But it *does* go away. Just avoid the fumes while they last.

Help! My soap molds are sitting on the counter, getting cold, and the soap isn't hardening!

This sometimes happens with Warm Technique soaps. If you move the soap molds to a warmer place—about the temperature you'd use if you were setting bread dough aside to rise—the soap will begin to saponify again, none the worse for its little vacation. You probably can find such a place—maybe near a heating vent, inside a gas oven with a pilot light, or by a window in direct sunlight. Or you can make one—maybe in a box with a heating pad turned on low. To help hold in the heat, you can cover the mold with a light cloth or some plastic wrap.

Help! My soap molds are sitting on the counter, getting warmer, but the soap is getting softer!

Cold Technique soaps will seem to have hardened when you take them from the refrigerator, but that's partly just thickening of the fat. As they warm up, they'll re-soften to some extent, but will then slowly harden again as saponification continues.

Help! My soap is covered with white powder!

Your first step is to test the powder with pH strips to make sure it's not lye. It probably isn't, but this is a "better safe than sorry" move that you definitely shouldn't skip.

If the powder isn't caustic, it's probably what soapmakers call soda ash. That's caused by reaction of the soap with air while saponifying. Some people only have problems with soda ash under certain weather conditions. Some say that specific ingredients seem to cause it. Others report a constant problem. You can ignore the ash, remove it, or take steps to prevent it.

If the soap's for your own use, it's fine to ignore any soda ash. It will wash off the first time you use the soap.

Soda ash can also be removed by scraping or slicing off the soap surface. The best tool I've found for this is a cheese slicer. Or you can remove the powder with a paper towel soaked with 99% isopropyl alcohol (sometimes incorrectly called "rubbing alcohol"). But neither of these measures is good for soaps made in fancy patterned molds.

To prevent soda ash, you must keep the hardening soap out of contact with the air. Right after pouring, lay plastic wrap over the soap surface, working out air bubbles and wrinkles. When the soap has hardened, remove it from the mold and wrap it all over tightly in more plastic wrap. Leave it that way for a couple of days. By then, the surface should have stopped being reactive.

Since this extends the setting and curing time a good deal, I wouldn't do it unless I knew a problem was likely.

Can I use "cold process oven process" (CPOP) on milk soaps?

In a word, no. I tried putting my soap in the oven after pouring and got a very ugly surface texture.

Can I convert a water-based soap recipe to make milk soap?

You can—but it may not be an improvement. I tried substituting milk for water in quite a few of my own recipes, and sometimes they didn't lather as well. On the other hand, some of the soaps were much better with milk. I didn't find any reliable way to predict it.

So, if you have a favorite recipe and want to try it with milk, go ahead—but regard the batch as an experiment. If you're using milk that's very high in fat, you may want to reduce your other superfatting a bit—but I suggest making one batch with the normal amount before you decide. Milk fat is never a large percentage of the total fat in a soap, so it probably won't push your recipe beyond the desirable range for superfatting.

Which makes lighter-colored soaps—Cool Technique or Warm Technique?

By logic, you'd think it would be Cool Technique. In my tests, though, they were about the same, provided I carefully followed the steps I've described. But don't think you can skip the chilling of Cool Technique soaps and have them come out as pale.

It's possible that the way powdered milk is dried makes its color more stable. I can't give all the reasons my batches came out as they did—I can only report the results.

Author Online!

For updates and more resources,
visit Anne's Soapmaking Page at

www.annelwatson.com/soapmaking

Resources on the Web

Anne's Soapmaking Page

Check here for the latest results of my experiments in soapmaking. There's always more to try and to learn!

www.annelwatson.com/soapmaking

A Campaign for Real Milk

Promotes raw milk and small-scale dairying. Find sources of farm milk for soapmaking in many parts of the world.

www.realmilk.com

Majestic Mountain Sage—Lye Calculator

For checking soap recipes and designing your own.

www.thesage.com/calcs

Marge's Soap House

Experiments with color and chocolate in milk soaps.

www.marges-soap-house.com

Index

About the Author

Anne L. Watson is the author of the wildly popular and widely acclaimed beginners book *Smart Soapmaking*. She has made soap professionally under the company name Soap Tree and before her retirement was a historic preservation architecture consultant. Her other published books include two novels, *Pacific Avenue* and *Skeeter: A Cat Tale*. Anne, her husband, Aaron, and their cat, Skeeter, live in Olympia, Washington. You can visit her at **www.annelwatson.com**.

CPSIA information can be obtained
at www.ICGtesting.com
Printed in the USA
LVOW05s1548191216
517948LV00020B/845/P